THE LOS ANGELES CLIPPERS

BY
MARK STEWART

NORWOODHOUSE PRESS

Norwood House Press
2544 Clinton Street
Buffalo, NY 14224

All photos including cover courtesy of Getty images, except: Topps, Inc. (7, 15, 20, 34 left,
35 left, 42 both), Century Publishing (16), Author's Collection (23, 25, 29, 35 right), Sports Illustrated
for Kids (24), SLAM Magazine (30), Star Co. (34 right, 37, 41).

The memorabilia, artifacts, and media images that are pictured in this book are presented for
educational and informational purposes and come from the collection of the author.

Art Director: Lisa Miley
Series Design: Ron Jaffe
Project Management: Upper Case Editorial Services LLC
Special thanks to Topps, Inc.

Names: Stewart, Mark, 1960 July 7-.
Title: The Los Angeles Clippers / Mark Stewart.
Description: Buffalo, NY : Norwood House Press, 2025. | Series: Team spirit |
Includes glossary and index.
Identifiers: ISBN 978-1-6845-0084-0 (pbk.) | ISBN 978-1-6845-0085-7 (library
bound) | ISBN 978-1-6845-0086-4 (ebook)
Subjects: LCSH: Los Angeles Clippers (Basketball team)--Juvenile literature. |
Basketball--California--Los Angeles--History--Juvenile literature.
Classification: LCC GV885.52.L65 S84 2025 | DDC 796.323'640979494--dc23

378N—022324
Manufactured in the United States of America in North Mankato, Minnesota.

TABLE OF CONTENTS

ABOUT OUR GLOSSARY

In this book, there may be several words that you are reading for the first time. Some are sports words, some are new vocabulary words, and some are familiar words that are used in an unusual way. All of these words are defined on page 46. Throughout the book, sports words appear in **bold type**. Regular vocabulary words appear in ***bold italic type***.

MAKING THE CLIPPERS

Not many sports teams can say they have called three cities home. The Clippers are one of those teams. They played their first season under a different name 2,500 miles away from Los Angeles, California—and made a stop on their way to L.A. All three places did have one thing in common: Each was home to basketball fans whose *spirits* rose and fell with the ups and downs of the team.

To make the Clippers, a player must be willing to give 100 percent to those fans, win or lose, game in and game out. Perhaps that is why the team has always found athletes with great skills and also big personalities. They love to hear the roar of the crowd when they make a game-changing play.

This book tells the story of the Clippers. They not only play against the other teams in the **National Basketball Association (NBA)**. They also compete with teams in other sports—and with teams in their own sport—in their sports-crazy city.

Kawhi Leonard and Paul George go "up-top" after bringing the fans to their feet. They rank among the greatest players in team history.

BUILDING BLOCKS

The Clippers began their basketball journey to Los Angeles far to the east, in Buffalo, New York. They joined the NBA as the Buffalo Braves for the 1970–71 season. The team's first star was Bob Kauffman. He was a strong forward with a smooth outside shot. The team's first coach was Dolph Schayes. He had been a star player for the Syracuse Nationals (now Philadelphia 76ers). Like Buffalo, Syracuse is a city in western New York State.

During the early 1970s, the Braves added more good players, including Bob McAdoo and Randy Smith. McAdoo was an unstoppable scorer who played forward and center. Few big men have ever shot as well. Smith was one of the quickest guards in the NBA and also one of the toughest. He set a league record by playing in 906 games in a row. With McAdoo and Smith leading the way, the Braves made it to the playoffs three years in a row from 1973–74 to 1975–76.

Unfortunately, the team always ran into an opponent with more skill and experience. Buffalo won only one postseason series during that period.

In 1978, the owner of the Braves, John Y. Brown, traded teams with Irv Levin, the owner of the Boston Celtics. Brown had owned the Kentucky Colonels, one of the best teams in the old **American Basketball Association (ABA)**. He loved the idea of owning the mighty Celtics. Levin preferred

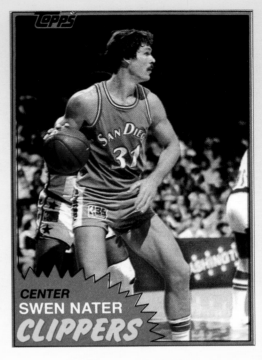

CENTER
SWEN NATER
CLIPPERS

to own a team in his home state of California. So he moved the Braves to the city of San Diego and renamed them the Clippers. A Clipper is an old-time sailing ship.

The Clippers won 43 games in 1978–79. Their top players included Randy Smith, World B. Free, Freeman Williams, and Swen Nater. Free finished second in the league in scoring. The following year, Bill Walton joined the Clippers. The fans in San Diego were very excited to have the star center. However, injuries kept Walton off the court for most of his time with the Clippers.

LEFT: Bob McAdoo shoots over Wes Unseld in a battle of two 1970s superstars. They played together for five seasons and rank among the brightest stars in team history.
ABOVE: Swen Nater looks for an open man on this 1981–82 trading card. He was one of the team's most popular players.

The Clippers moved north to Los Angeles for the 1984–85 season. Derek Smith, Norm Nixon, and Marques Johnson starred for the team over the next few years. However, the Clippers' luck did not improve until the 1990s, when they made it to the playoffs three times. The team had several good players during the '90s, including Ken Norman, Charles Smith, Danny Manning, Loy Vaught, Ron Harper, Lamond Murray, and Eric Piatkowski.

The person who helped build the Clippers into a solid team was Elgin Baylor. Southern California basketball fans remembered Baylor during his years as an All-Star with the Los Angeles Lakers. The Clippers hired the Hall of Famer to run the club's business.

Toward the end of the 1990s, the Clippers decided to rebuild their team. It took many years to put a winning group together, but after nine losing seasons, Los Angeles returned to the playoffs. The team's leaders were a pair of forwards, Elton Brand and Corey Maggette. They had been teammates at Duke University. The challenge the Clippers faced was finding players to help Brand and Maggette. Before they could, the two stars left L.A. to play for more successful teams. Once again, Clippers fans were left to wait and wonder when they might cheer for a winning team again.

That day came sooner than many experts thought. In 2010, the

Corey Maggette rises toward the basket in a game against the Phoenix Suns.

Clippers **drafted** Blake Griffin. Griffin was a forward with great strength and *outrageous* leaping ability. In 2011, the team traded for Chris Paul, an **All-Star** guard, and signed *veterans* Caron Butler and Chauncey Billups. They teamed with DeAndre Jordan, a *rugged* center who become the NBA's top rebounder.

This group came within one victory of winning the Pacific Division in 2011–12. More important, they brought a winning attitude to the Clippers that continues to this day. Their favorite play was the rim-rattling **alley-oop**. Los Angeles fans called this offense "Lob City." No team was more fun to watch. More importantly, the Clippers became a team that good players wanted to join. In the years that followed, their stars included Montrezl Harrell, Ivica Zubac, Danilo Gallinari, Lou Williams, JJ Reddick, Jamal Crawford, Paul George, and Kawhi Leonard. In 2020–21, Leonard and George led the Clippers to the Western Conference Finals for the first time in team history. They fell two wins short of their first trip the **NBA Finals**.

Reaching the championship series is the goal of every team, of course. The Clippers have had to wait longer than anyone imagined when they joined the league as the Braves in 1970. For their Los Angeles fans, that just means that first trip to the finals will be an extra-special one.

Blake Griffin leaps over a car during the 2011 NBA Slam Dunk Contest. Griffin's jumping ability made him a sensation around the NBA.

GAME DAY

When the Clippers played in Buffalo as the Braves, their home court was the Buffalo Memorial Auditorium. Fans called it "The Aud" for short. The Braves shared the arena with the Buffalo Sabres hockey team. When the team moved west, it made its next home in the San Diego Sports Arena.

After six years in San Diego, the Clippers moved two hours north and played their home games in the Los Angeles Memorial Sports Arena. The Lakers had played there for many years after moving to Los Angeles in 1960. In 1999, the Clippers and Lakers both moved into a new arena, which they share with the Sparks of the **Women's National Basketball Association (WNBA)** and the Kings hockey team.

BY THE NUMBERS

- There are 19,079 seats for basketball in the Clippers' arena.
- The arena is also used for political events, ice skating shows, and music concerts. Nearly 4,000,000 people visit the building each year.
- The arena has hosted the finals of the League of Legends e-sports world championship twice.

The Clippers play against Kobe Bryant and the Lakers in the arena they still share. In 2020, Bryant died in a helicopter crash. Now there is a statue of him outside the arena.

TEAM COLORS

The team colors of the Buffalo Braves started as black, white, and orange. The team *logo* included a feather from a Native American headdress. In 1973–74, the Braves switched their main color to light blue. When the team moved to California and became the Clippers, it changed its logo to show a clipper ship, but continued to use light blue on their uniforms.

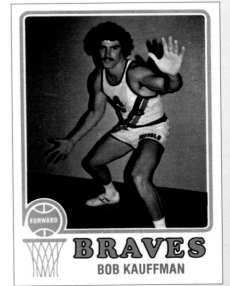

Over the years, the Clippers have experimented with different shades of blue. They used a dark blue after moving to Los Angeles in 1984. In the late 1980s, the Clippers switched to red as their main color. Since then, they have used different combinations of red, white, blue, silver, and black. The team's name and city are spelled out in several different styles of lettering.

LEFT: Russell Westbrook, Paul George, and Kawhi Leonard wear the team's red-white-and blue jerseys. All three may one day represent the team in the Basketball Hall of Fame. **ABOVE**: Bob Kauffman wears the original black, white, and orange uniform of the Braves.

LAST TEAM STANDING

Bad luck and good opponents are a fact of life in the NBA playoffs. The last team standing in the NBA Finals is the one that raises its game and gets a few lucky bounces. The Buffalo Braves and Los Angeles Clippers have put some excellent players on the court for the postseason—and have had clubs with enough talent to win it all. However, as of 2023–24, the club was still waiting for its first trip to the championship series.

In 1974 and again in 1975, Bob McAdoo and the Braves battled

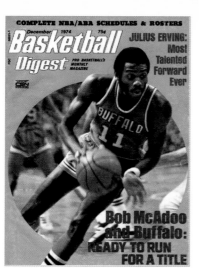

to the **deciding game** of their series against the Boston Celtics and Washington Bullets (now Wizards). The Braves fell just short both times—and then had to watch as Boston and Washington went all the way to the NBA Finals. In 1976, the Braves won a playoff series for the first time. They defeated the Philadelphia 76ers, and McAdoo was a one-man show in the last game. He scored 51 points and had 22 rebounds in a thrilling 124–123

Bob McAdoo was ready for a run at the title in the 1970s . . . but the Braves fell short.

overtime victory. Unfortunately, Buffalo ran into the red-hot Celtics after that. They lost the series in six games. As in 1974, Boston went on to win the NBA championship.

No one knew it then, but the team's next playoff *triumph* would not come until 2006. They were now the Los Angeles Clippers and they had an exciting team that starred Elton Brand and Corey Maggette. Chris Kaman, Sam Cassell, Cuttino Mobley, and Shaun Livingston also played key roles. The Clippers beat the high-scoring Denver Nuggets and then faced the Phoenix Suns. Almost everyone picked the Suns to win, but the Clippers won three times and pushed Phoenix to a Game 7. Brand scored 36 points, but his effort was not enough and the Suns escaped to play another day.

The Clippers made the playoffs almost every year starting in 2012. They often won in the opening round but failed to advance after that. In 2020–21, Los Angeles made Tyronn Lue its new head coach. The team gave him a ton of experienced talent to work with. Kawhi Leonard and Paul George were two of the best forwards in the NBA. Six other players saw time in the starting lineup, including Nicolas Batum, Marcus Morris, Reggie Jackson, and Patrick Beverley.

Elton Brand makes a move against the Nuggets in the 2006 playoffs.

The Clippers won 47 games in 2020–21 and went into the playoffs with high hopes. Their fans could hardly believe it when they lost their first two games at home against Luka Doncic and the Dallas Mavericks. The Clippers *recovered* to win two of the next three games. In Game 6, Leonard scored 45 points to help Los Angeles tie the series. He and George were sensational in Game 7 and the Clippers won, 126–111.

Next up were the Utah Jazz. Incredibly, the Clippers lost the first two games again. Even more incredible, they won the next four in a row to take the series and advance to the Western Conference Finals for the first time. They also became the first playoff team in history to come back to win twice in a row after falling behind 2 games to 0.

Unfortunately, bad luck and a good opponent caught up with the Clippers before they had a chance to play in the NBA Finals. Leonard suffered a knee injury during the series against Utah and was unable to play in in the conference finals series against their old foes, the Suns.

Los Angeles lost the first two games again, but this time it was too steep a hill to climb and they lost, 4 games to 2. It was another dark cloud in team history, but this time there was a silver lining: The Clippers proved they had the toughness and talent to win in the playoffs when the odds are against them.

Kawhi Leonard and Marcus Morris trap Luka Doncic of the Mavericks during the 2021 playoffs.

LEADING LIGHTS

Some players lead with their words. Others lead with their actions. The greatest Braves and Clippers inspired their teammates and thrilled their fans by doing both. They are the team's brightest stars.

RANDY SMITH   6´3˝ Guard

• BORN: 12/12/1948   • DIED: 6/4/2009   • PLAYED FOR TEAM: 1971–72 TO 1978–79

Randy Smith began his career as a forward. When the Braves moved him to guard, he became one of the best players in the NBA. Smith used his soft jump shot to average 20 points a game four years in a row during the 1970s.

BRAVES
RANDY SMITH

BOB MCADOO   6´9˝ Center/Forward

• BORN: 9/25/1951

• PLAYED FOR TEAM: 1972–73 TO 1976–77

Bob McAdoo might have been the best-shooting big man in basketball history. He had a quick release and a smooth touch. McAdoo led the NBA in scoring three times and was named the league's Most Valuable Player (MVP) in 1974–75.

ERNIE DiGREGORIO   6´ 0˝ Guard

• BORN: 1/15/1951   • PLAYED FOR TEAM: 1973–74 TO 1976–77

Everyone knew Ernie DiGregorio as "Ernie D." He was one of the smartest passers in the league. When he and Randy Smith formed Buffalo's **backcourt**, the Braves were tough to beat. DiGregorio was also an excellent free-throw shooter.

JIM MCMILLIAN   6´ 5˝ Forward

• BORN: 3/11/1948   • DIED: 5/16/2016   • PLAYED FOR TEAM: 1973–74 TO 1975–76

Jim McMillian brought a winning attitude to the Braves. He had *previously* been a member of the NBA champion Los Angeles Lakers. In McMillian's three years in Buffalo, the team won 134 games.

WORLD B. FREE   6´ 3˝ Guard

• BORN: 12/9/1955

• PLAYED FOR TEAM: 1978–79 TO 1979–80

Although World Free only played two years with the club, he left his mark on the Clippers with his wonderful skill and creativity. He was the number-two scorer in the NBA both seasons and did things on the court that fans talked about for years. Free's one-on-one battles with top defenders were great fun to watch.

LEFT: Randy Smith
ABOVE: World B. Free

BILL WALTON 6′ 11″ Center

• BORN: 11/5/1952   • DIED: 5/27/2024   • PLAYED FOR TEAM: 1979–80 TO 1984–85

Clippers fans still talk about what might have been had Bill Walton stayed healthy. Unfortunately, in six seasons with the team, he played only 169 games. When Walton was on the court for the Clippers, he was one of the most brilliant centers in history.

DANNY MANNING 6′ 10″ Forward

• BORN: 5/17/1966

• PLAYED FOR TEAM: 1988–89 TO 1993–94

The Clippers made Danny Manning the first pick in the 1988 **NBA draft**. He hurt his knee as a rookie, but came back to be one of the league's best all-around players. Manning represented the Clippers in the All-Star Game twice.

LOY VAUGHT 6′ 9″ Forward

• BORN: 2/27/1968

• PLAYED FOR TEAM: 1990–91 TO 1997–98

During the 1990s, Loy Vaught was the team's most dependable player. He was a good scorer and rebounder—and an even tougher competitor and leader.

ABOVE: Danny Manning drives to the basket.   **RIGHT**: Chris Kaman makes an opponent pay for getting too close to the basket. Kaman loves signing this photo.

COREY MAGGETTE   6′ 6″ Forward

- BORN: 11/12/1979 • PLAYED FOR TEAM: 2000–01 TO 2007–08

No one liked to guard Corey Maggette. He could make a monster dunk one time down the court, and then connect on a long 3-pointer the next. Maggette averaged more than 20 points a game three times for the Clippers.

ELTON BRAND   6′ 8″ Forward

- BORN: 3/11/1979 • PLAYED FOR TEAM: 2001–02 TO 2007–08

The Clippers were never known for paying their players a lot of money—until Elton Brand came along. He was worth every penny. Night in and night out, Brand scored 20 points and pulled down 10 rebounds, with plenty of blocks, assists, and steals.

CHRIS KAMAN   7′ 0″ Center

- BORN: 4/28/1982
- PLAYED FOR TEAM: 2003–04 TO 2010–11

The Clippers picked Chris Kaman in the first round of the 2003 NBA draft. Fans liked him immediately for his hard work and tough defense. Kaman did whatever it took to guard the basket.

DeANDRE JORDAN   6′ 11″ Center

- BORN: 7/21/1988
- PLAYED FOR TEAM: 2008–09 to 2017–18

DeAndre Jordan was a mountain of a man who was at his best playing close to the basket. He teamed with Blake Griffin and Chris Paul during the Clippers' "Lob City" days and was a good shot-blocker. Los Angeles fans loved Jordan. No matter how close the score was, he always seemed to be having the time of his life.

DeAndre Jordan
Center ★ Los Angeles Clippers

BLAKE GRIFFIN   6′ 9″ Forward

- BORN: 3/16/1989
- PLAYED FOR TEAM: 2010–11 To 2017–18

Blake Griffin's favorite play was *plucking* a pass out of the air and slamming it through the basket. He was the NBA Slam Dunk champion as a rookie and an All-Star five times for the Clippers.

CHRIS PAUL   6′ 0″ Guard

- BORN: 5/6/1985 • PLAYED FOR TEAM: 2011–12 to 2016–17

Chris Paul brought his fine all-around game to Los Angeles and turned the Clippers into one of the most thrilling teams in the NBA. His *pinpoint* passes led to rim-rattling dunks, while his defense drove opponents mad. In 2013–14, Paul fought through injuries to lead the Clippers to 57 wins—their most ever.

JAMAL CRAWFORD 6´ 5˝ Guard

- Born: 3/20/1980
- Played for Team: 2012–13 to 2016–17

When Jamal Crawford went on one of his famous hot streaks, no one was more fun to watch. He was a lightning-quick **ball-handler** and fearless shooter who came off the bench to lead many amazing comebacks.

KAWHI LEONARD 6´ 7˝ Forward

- Born: 6/29/1991
- First Season with Team: 2019–20

After winning championships with the Spurs and Raptors, Kawhi Leonard brought his winning ways to the Clippers. He set a personal best in his first season by averaging over 27 points a game. Leonard's quiet leadership and *superb* defense made Los Angeles one of the NBA's most feared teams.

PAUL GEORGE 6´ 8˝ Guard-Forward

- Born: 5/2/1990   • Played for Team: 2019–20 to 2023–24

Los Angeles fans hadn't seen a shooter as smooth as Paul George in a long time. But it was his all-around game that made them jump out of their seats. George set personal bests in assists and steals during his second season with the Clippers, while scoring 20 to 30 points most games.

LEFT: DeAndre Jordan
ABOVE: Jamal Crawford

X'S AND O'S

The Clippers have had some excellent coaches over the years. During their days as the Buffalo Braves, they enjoyed great success under Jack Ramsay. He later coached the Portland Trailblazers to the 1977 NBA Championship. In San Diego, the Clippers' coaches included Gene Shue and Paul Silas. Shue coached the Philadelphia 76ers against Ramsay in the 1977 NBA Finals and was named Coach of the Year twice. Silas had played in the NBA Finals as a member of the Boston Celtics and Seattle Supersonics (now the Oklahoma City Thunder).

In the years after the Clippers moved to Los Angeles, some of the NBA's best coaces worked on the sidelines for the team. Don Chaney, Larry Brown, Bill Fitch, and Mike Dunleavy all led the Clippers at one time or another. Dunleavy coached Los Angeles to 47 victories in 2005–06 and later set a team record for victories in a career.

Vinny del Negro and Doc Rivers were the coaches who got the Clippers back on the winning track after years of disappointment.

Mike Dunleavy was the Clippers career leader in victories.

They were followed by Tyronn Lue. Lue had coached the Cleveland Cavaliers to the NBA championship in 2016. In his first year on the sidelines, he led the Clippers to the conference finals.

Every boy or girl who ever picked up a basketball has dreamed of hitting a buzzer-beating jump shot in the playoffs to win a Game 7. Chris Paul lived that dream in 2015, when the Clippers played the San Antonio Spurs in the first round. Few people believed the Clippers would win more than a game or two. The Spurs were the *defending* world champions, after all. But here the Clippers were, in the deciding game, tied at 109–109 with less than ten seconds on the clock.

Paul got the ball just inside the halfcourt line and dribbled to his right. The Spurs knew he had an injured leg and Danny Green guarded him closely. Paul had already hit a 30-foot bomb to beat the buzzer at the end of the third quarter. Green did not want to let him do it again.

When Green got a little too close, Paul exploded past him. Paul left his feet and twisted to face the basket—only to find center Tim Duncan in his face. Duncan jumped as high as his could, putting

This is Chris Paul's favorite photo to autograph. It shows
his amazing buzzer-beater against the Spurs.

his long arm between Paul and the rim. Paul floated a shot over
Duncan that **kissed** off the backboard and went through the net for
a 111–109 victory.

WAIT . . . WHAT?

The Clippers once traded five first-round draft picks for one player. In the summer of 2019, the Clippers went shopping for

a game-changing two-way superstar. The Oklahoma City Thunder offered Paul George, but the price was incredibly high. Not only did the Clippers end up trading five first-round draft picks. They also sent two of their best players to the Thunder, Danilo Gallinari and Shai Gilgeous–Alexander. Clippers fans gave the trade a thumbs-up when George averaged over 20 points a game year after year. They also loved to watch his amazing work as a "perimeter defender"— a player who uses his balance and quickness to make opponents take longer shots than they would like.

ABOVE: When Paul George joined the Clippers, the trade made the front page of *SLAM Magazine.*

DID YOU KNOW?

The Clippers were almost the NBA's first team in Florida. In 1976, a wealthy Florida couple named the Cowans agreed on a handshake to buy the Buffalo Braves. They planned to move the club to the city of Hollywood, an hour north of Miami. Braves fans were furious, and the city of Buffalo tried to block the sale. The Cowans got nervous and walked away without buying the team.

DID YOU KNOW?

The subject of the Drake song "6 Man" played for the Clippers? Lou Williams had a long career in the NBA, including several seasons as the Clippers' "sixth man"—a player who comes off the bench to give his team a lift. In fact, Williams was named NBA Sixth Man of the Year three times, once with the Toronto Raptors and twice with the Clippers.

UNBELIEVABLE!

One of the hardest things to do in basketball is to make a comeback when you are the visiting team. It is even harder when your opponent is the number-one seed in the playoffs—and you are number eight. That was the scene in Game 2 of the 2019 first-round series between the Clippers and Golden State Warriors.

Midway through the third quarter, the Warriors held a 94–63 lead. Their best shooter, Steph Curry, took a seat on the bench to rest for Game 3. No one thought the Clippers could come back. But Golden State's All-Star forward, Kevin Durant, began to turn the ball over. The Clippers starting playing better defense and began hitting their shots. By the end of the third quarter, they had cut the lead to 17—but still had a long way to go against a great team.

In the fourth quarter, the Clippers kept up the pressure and the Warriors began to panic. They made poor passes, took bad shots, and lost their focus on defense. Meanwhile, the Clippers just kept pouring it on. They had already made two huge comebacks on the road earlier in the year, and realized they had a chance to make history.

Montrezl Harrell cannot contain his excitement as the Clippers pull off their great comeback against the Warriors.

And they did. The Clippers took the lead with time running out in the fourth quarter and held on to win, 135–131. Their 31-point comeback set a new record for the playoffs.

For a history-making comeback, you have to have one player who cannot miss. For the Clippers, that player was Lou Williams. He scored 29 of his 36 points in the second half. Williams also had 11 assists. Twice he missed shots but *scrambled* to grab the rebound—and then make the follow-up shot.

Another hero was Landry Shamet. He only scored 12 points, but all of his baskets were 3-pointers—including the long-range shot that sealed the victory with under a minute left. The defensive hero for Los Angeles was Patrick Beverley, who made great plays against Curry and Durant.

After the game, coach Doc Rivers congratulated his players and joked, "We are roaches! They can't kill us!"

IT'S ABOUT TIME

The basketball season is played from October through June. That means each season takes place at the end of one year and the beginning of the next. In this timeline, the accomplishments of the Braves and Clippers are shown by season.

1970-71
The team joins the NBA as the Buffalo Braves.

1978-79
The team moves to San Diego and becomes the Clippers.

1984-85
The Clippers move to Los Angeles.

1975-77
Bob McAdoo is named league MVP.

1983-84
Bill Walton sets a team record with 10 blocked shots in a game.

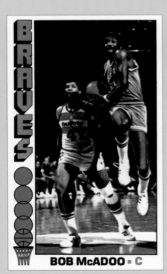
BOB McADOO • C

Bob McAdoo

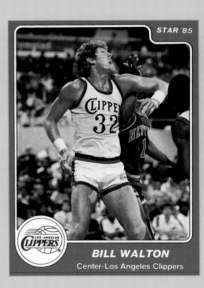
STAR '85
BILL WALTON
Center-Los Angeles Clippers

Bill Walton

Danny Manning

A signed photo of Blake Griffin with his Rookie of the Year award.

1988-89
The Clippers choose Danny Manning with the first pick in the draft.

2010-11
Blake Griffin is named NBA Rookie of the Year

2021-22
The team reaches the conference finals for the first time.

1990-91
Charles Smith ties the team record with 52 points in a game.

2003-04
Quentin Richardson makes eight 3-pointers in a game.

Quentin Richardson

THAT'S A FACT

CALIFORNIA KIDS

In 2023–24, the Clippers added all-time greats James Harden and Russell Westbrook to a roster that already included Kawhi Leonard and Paul George. All four superstars grew up in the Los Angeles area.

AND BINGO WAS HIS NAME-O

When a Clipper makes a 3-point shot, cries of "Bingo!" can be heard around the arena. The tradition was started by announcer Ralph Lawler in their first year in California, when Bobby "Bingo" Smith thrilled fans with his 3-point shooting.

FORGET ME NOT

Bob McAdoo was the NBA's best player in the mid-1970s. He was also the most forgetful. When the Braves were on the road, he was famous for leaving his stuff in hotels—including the basketball shoes he needed to wear for the game.

HAIL TO THE CHIEF

In 2013, Chris Paul was elected president of the NBA Players Association. Paul worked hard for players' rights and pushed to make Michele Roberts the Executive Director. She became the first woman to head a major sports *union* in the United States.

MR. CLEAN

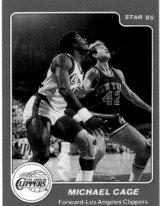

Michael Cage was the Clippers' best rebounder during the 1980s. His nickname was "*Windex* Man" because he rebounded—or "cleaned the glass"—so well. Cage led the NBA in rebounds per game in 1987–88.

DREAMING BIG

In the early 1980s, one of the Clippers' best players was Joe Bryant. His young son told his dad's teammates that one day he too would play in the NBA. The young man kept his word. His name was Kobe Bryant.

ALL-TIME GREATS

In 2021, the NBA announced history's greatest 75 players in honor of its 75th Anniversary. Of the 11 active players on the list, two were beloved Clippers Kawhi Leonard and Chris Paul.

LEFT: Ralph Lawler **ABOVE**: Michael Cage

SPEAKING OF BASKETBALL

"We respected him . . . we idolized him so much."

▶ **MARQUES JOHNSON,** *on Clippers General Manager and Hall of Famer Elgin Baylor*

"I was a scorer. I was a scorer deluxe. I tried to get every rebound and block anything close to the basket. I tried my best to be an all-around player."

▶ **BOB McADOO,** *on how he became an MVP*

"Every **setback** is an opportunity for a comeback."

▶ **TYRONN LUE,** *on how he keeps the Clippers focused during games*

"I started to figure out that I could have a bad three quarters and still have a strong fourth, still win, still do things to help our team."

▶ **BLAKE GRIFFIN,** *on the difference experience makes*

"When we don't communicate, we get our butts whipped. It's that simple."

▶ **SAM CASSELL,** *on the importance of talking to teammates throughout a game*

"Usually I've had two jobs—be the best defender and the best scorer."

▶ **PAUL GEORGE,** *on the pressure of being a two-way player*

"I just keep pushing to the fourth quarter until it finally ends."

▶ **KAWHI LEONARD,** *on the effort it takes to be a great defender*

"You work hard and stick with it…good things will happen. That's what I'm a believer of."

▶ **ELTON BRAND,** *on leading the Clippers to the playoffs*

LEFT: Elgin Baylor
ABOVE: Sam Cassell

ROAD TRIP

For fans of the Clippers, all roads lead to Los Angeles. But each journey begins somewhere else. Match the pushpins on these maps to the Team Facts, and you will discover the ultimate Clippers road trip!

TEAM FACTS

1. **LOS ANGELES, CALIFORNIA**—The Clippers have played here since 1984–85.
2. **BUFFALO, NEW YORK**—The team played here as the Braves from 1970–71 to 1977–78.
3. **SAN DIEGO, CALIFORNIA**—The Clippers moved here in 1978–79.
4. **HATTIESBURG, MISSISSIPPI**—Danny Manning was born here.
5. **MACON, GEORGIA**—Norm Nixon was born here.
6. **WEST MEMPHIS, ARKANSAS**—Michael Cage was born here.
7. **MELROSE PARK, ILLINOIS**—Corey Maggette was born here.
8. **GRAND RAPIDS, MICHIGAN**—Loy Vaught was born here.
9. **BROOKLYN, NEW YORK**—Mike Dunleavy was born here.
10. **PHILADELPHIA, PENNSYLVANIA**—Jack Ramsay was born here.
11. **GREENSBORO, NORTH CAROLINA**—Bob McAdoo was born here.
12. **SAINT'ANGELO LODIGIANO, ITALY**—Danilo Gallinari was born here.
13. **MOSTAR, BOSNIA AND HERZEGOVINA**—Ivica Zubac was born here.

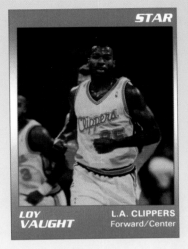

Loy Vaught

HONOR ROLL

The great Braves and Clippers players have left their marks on the record books. These are the best of the best!

ERNIE DiGREGORIO • G

CLIPPERS AWARD WINNERS

ROOKIE OF THE YEAR		COMEBACK PLAYER OF THE YEAR	
Bob McAdoo	1972–73	Marques Johnson	1985–86
Ernie DiGregorio	1973–74	**NBA MVP**	
Adrian Dantley	1976–77	Bob McAdoo	1974–75
Terry Cummings	1982–83		
Blake Griffin	2010–11	**SLAM DUNK CHAMPION**	
		Brent Barry	1995–96
SIXTH MAN OF THE YEAR		Blake Griffin	2010–11
Jamal Crawford	2013–14		
Jamal Crawford	2015–16	**ALL-STAR GAME MVP**	
Lou Williams	2017–18	Chris Paul	2012–13
Lou Williams	2018–19	Kawhi Leonard	2019–20
Montrezl Harrell	2019–20		

BRAVES
BOB McADOO

TOP LEFT: Ernie DiGregorio
BOTTOM LEFT: Bob McAdoo
RIGHT: Brent Barry in action during the 1996 Slam Dunk Contest.

NOTHING BUT NET

When a Los Angeles Clipper takes aim at the basket, fans hope he hits nothing but net. That is one way of describing a perfect shot in basketball. It does not touch the backboard or the rim and makes a swishing sound that is music to a player's ears. In the NBA, defense is important, but scoring is the name of the game.

During the team's early years as the Buffalo Braves, Bob McAdoo was the NBA's most feared scorer. Most players his size positioned themselves near the basket and waited for a pass and an easy shot. McAdoo could score from almost anywhere on the court. He had a *feathery* backspin jump shot that often kissed the rim and backboard before going through the hoop. In 1974–75, McAdoo led the league with 2,831 points to set a team record that has yet to be broken. Not surprisingly, McAdoo also set the team record for points in a game. In 1974, he scored 52 against the Boston Celtics. Two years later, he tied his own mark with 52 against the Seattle Supersonics.

That record was McAdoo's alone until 1990, when Charles Smith of the Clippers tied it with 52 points against the Nuggets. Smith had watched the team play the night before and noticed that the Denver defense was leaving his favorite spot wide open.

"I figured out from that game what would work," Smith remembers. "I told the guards to get me the ball."

The team record for most point in a playoff game also belongs to McAdoo. In 1975, he dropped 50 on the Washington Bullets. The Braves won the game but lost the series in seven games. McAdoo scored more than 30 points in every contest.

Charles Smith looks for an opening in the defense. He was unstoppable against the Denver Nuggets in December of 1990.

BASKETBALL WORDS

ALL-STAR—A player recognized as being among the best in the league, who is chosen for the annual NBA All-Star Game.

ALLEY-OOP—A play where one player throws the ball high enough for his teammate to catch it and dunk before landing.

AMERICAN BASKETBALL ASSOCIATION (ABA)—A professional league that played from 1967–68 to 1975–76. Four ABA teams joined the NBA for the 1976–77 season.

BACKCOURT—A term for a team's guards.

BALL-HANDLER—A player with dribbling and passing skills.

DECIDING GAME—The last contest of a series that is tied.

DRAFTED—Selected from the best college players. The NBA draft is held each June.

KISSED—Gently brushed against the rim or backboard.

NATIONAL BASKETBALL ASSOCIATION (NBA)—A professional league that began in 1946 as the Basketball Association of America and changed its name after merging with the National Basketball League in 1949.

NBA DRAFT—A yearly event where teams pick from the best college and overseas players.

NBA FINALS—The championship series of professional basketball.

NBA PLAYERS ASSOCIATION—An organization that fights for the interests of players.

OVERTIME—The five-minute period played after a game is tied.

PACIFIC DIVISION—A group of teams that play near the West Coast of the United States.

PLAYOFFS—The games played after the regular season that lead to the championship finals.

POSTSEASON—The games played after the regular season, including the playoffs and NBA Finals.

NUMBER-ONE SEED—A team placed in the top spot during the postseason.

RELEASE—The way a player lets go of the basketball when he shoots.

ROOKIE—A player in his first professional season.

WESTERN CONFERENCE FINALS—The postseason series that decides one of the teams to play in the NBA Finals.

WOMEN'S NATIONAL BASKETBALL ASSOCIATION (WNBA)—A professional league that played its for season in 1997.

VOCABULARY WORDS

DEFENDING—Previous.

FEATHERY—Light and soft.

LOGO—A design or symbol used by a business.

OUTRAGEOUS—Startling and out of the ordinary.

PINPOINT—Fine and precise.

PLUCKING—Quickly removing an object.

PREVIOUSLY—At an earlier time.

RECOVERED—Bounced back after a poor performance.

RUGGED—Tough and determined.

SCRAMBLED—Moved quickly and suddenly.

SETBACK—A stop in progress.

SPIRITS—The mood or emotions of a group.

SUPERB—Excellent and impressive.

TRIUMPH—A great victory.

UNION—A group formed by people who share a purpose or profession.

VETERANS—People with a lot of experience.

WINDEX—The name of a glass-cleaning spray.

ABOUT THE AUTHOR

MARK STEWART has written more than 50 books for kids on pro and college basketball. He grew up in New York City rooting for the Knicks and Nets, and was lucky enough to meet many of the players on those teams. He comes from a publishing family. His parents edited and wrote for national magazines and his grandfather was Sunday Editor of *The New York Times*. After graduating with a degree in history from Duke University, Mark wrote for sports and lifestyle magazines and published his first book in 1992. Since then, he has profiled more than 1,000 athletes, many of whom were Braves and Clippers—including Chauncey Billups, Elton Brand, James Harden, Corey Maggette, Bob McAdoo, Chris Paul, and Bill Walton. Mark also worked with Chris Paul on a Hall of Fame project with the NBA Players Association.

ON THE ROAD

LOS ANGELES CLIPPERS
1111 South Figueroa Street
Los Angeles, California 90005

NAISMITH BASKETBALL HALL OF FAME
1000 Hall of Fame Avenue
Springfield, Massachusetts 01105

ON THE BOOKSHELF

To learn more about the sport of basketball, look for these books at your library or bookstore:

- Berglund, Bruce. *Basketball GOATs: The Greatest Athletes of All Time.* North Mankato, MN: Capstone Press, 2021.

- Flynn, Brendan. *The Genius Kid's Guide to Pro Basketball.* Mendota Heights, MN: North Star Editions, 2022.

- Peel, Dan. *NBA Legends: Discover Basketball's All-time Greats.* Chicago, IL: Sona Books, 2021.

INDEX

PAGE NUMBERS IN **BOLD** REFER TO ILLUSTRATIONS.